Make Yourself Happier

Simple Ways to Stop Negative Thinking

By Tim Harris

With an Honours degree from London University, specialising in the Psychology of Education, Tim Harris spent most of his career supporting adults. He became very interested in what obstructs people from learning, and the negative views people have of themselves. He trained as a counsellor and came to realise that most obstacles to learning are in our own heads. He also learned that people can change their behaviour and, particularly, the way they think about themselves.

After running very successful Positive Living classes for many years, Tim has decided to write down what has worked well with his groups. He has translated Psychology, and all of its jargon, into plain English. The exercises and advice are easy to follow. His courses have produced excellent results.

Contents

How did we get here?

Covid-19 and Isolation

Things people have said about this course

Chapter 1   Negative Thinking 1

Chapter 2   Negative Thinking 2

Chapter 3   Are you struggling?

Chapter 4   Me time

Chapter 5   Brain rest

Chapter 6   Gratitude/Appreciation

Chapter 7   Looking outwards

Chapter 8   Learn a positive description of yourself

Chapter 9   What have we learned?

Chapter 10 Where else can I get support?

How did we get here?

I'm home from work. I have closed the front door and locked it. And that one everyday action says I am shutting the world out, locking myself inside my safe little home where nothing unexpected will happen, because I am in charge. The trouble is, when I am in company, I want to be alone, but, when I am alone, I want to be in company.

OK, don't go down that negative thinking route again, Tim; let's get on with it. Put the kettle on, check the garden, check the post, put the news on, drink my tea, smoke a cigarette, think about food. Beans on toast with grated cheese, maybe fry up some mushrooms. Plenty of protein, plenty of fibre, a bit of veg. Another cig, more tea. It's getting dark now, a little cold. I really am alone, alone with my thoughts and the TV until bedtime. It's been like this for years. Oh, stop being so miserable. Where's the 'remote'?

Great, Wednesday, Champions' League. Have I got any chocolate? No, but I have got two beers, one for each half, then bed. Get a cushion to support my lower back, make myself cumfy and let the night's entertainment begin.

I was a bit rude to Jackie today. I shouldn't have snapped. I don't like it when people say they'll do things and they don't. No, that's no excuse. I'll apologise tomorrow. I wonder what people think of me. Am I harsh? I don't think so. What do they really think of me? What could I do to make them like me more? Nobody ever calls. Perhaps nobody likes me. Maybe my friends are just being polite when they see me. Do I like myself? Not much. Was I a good dad? Nope. Well, sometimes I was but not when Shelley was struggling in her teens, not when I lost Jake in Spain, or when he fell out of his high cabin bed because I hadn't fixed the restraining rail yet. Oh Jesus, I still shudder at that. I've got that empty feeling in my stomach. It feels tense like it needs something. Some company, some hugs, some laughter, some love, maybe. Seven billion people on the planet and not one of them is with me. What do I do or say that is so wrong with me? I am a kind person. I look after a few people. Why does everybody else seem so happy and successful? OK, not everybody, but most of them.

Blimey it's half-time. That went quick. I remember the goal but that's all.

And the second half was spent pretty much the same way as the first. Lots of questions and memories, all negative. Then some TV channel-hopping for an hour. Then bed. Last night was the same, and the night before, and tomorrow will be. Night after night, I sit there beating myself up with no idea how to stop it.

Negative thinking is like an epidemic these days. It is the most common symptom of people with problems. Loneliness, relationship problems, stress at work and at home, not liking yourself, not coping, physical illness, mental health problems, drinking too much, and so many other things can lead us into quite a negative view of life. Several of my students have described the feeling of being trapped, as if in a jail, unable to break out of their gloom

For some of us, depression is like a partner we have got used to living with but don't particularly like and can't get rid of. The past is like a magnet pulling our minds back to bad memories, with low opinions of ourselves, lack of confidence, a gloomy view of life and not getting very much done. Living in the future can be difficult, too. Anxiety sufferers can devote their thinking time to fear of things which haven't even happened yet. 'What if this happens, or that? What if I fail? What if they say no? What if I, or my kids, get hurt? I can't cope.' And they miss the first half of the football, too, drowning in needless, unwanted, unproductive thoughts and worries.

Anxiety and depression: two scourges of modern times which affect so many of us. And both illnesses seem to isolate sufferers from the rest of the world with only negative thoughts for company. Learning how to minimise negative thinking, and live more positively, will bring significant improvements to your life.

There are techniques, simple ones, which can reduce the amount of time you spend in misery. You can manage your thoughts much better than you do at the moment. This book will show you how. It is not about curing depression and anxiety: it is more about helping you manage them better and being less of a victim.

I had a few relationships with women. At the start of them, all my troubles were forgotten, but slowly the same old thoughts would start to creep back in. I still spent plenty of nights on my own. The initial buzz of meeting someone new began to wear off, the negative thoughts returned, and I started to realise the solution to my problems wasn't in meeting someone else. It was in me. I had to sort myself out.

I had travelled a lot and met some fascinating people from Australia and the USA where Happiness courses were becoming really big business. I researched some of these courses and learned that my happiness was in my own hands. I also learned that it was mostly common sense. We know we need to stop thinking the same old bad thoughts every day: we need to find times where we can switch off from life; we need to have more control of our minds; we need to look after our bodies better, and some of us will even admit that we need to get a life. Some of you would appreciate some ways of coping with depression, sleeplessness, anxiety, loneliness and bad memories. They are here in this book.

At Harvard University, an expert advertised a happiness course, and it became the most 'subscribed to' course in the history of the university. Yes, rich and highly intelligent people suffer too. You are not on your own. Huge numbers of people are having problems with negative thinking.

Because I was still feeling pretty depressed a lot of the time, I attended a course in Coventry, for people suffering from anxiety and depression, which turned out to be quite similar to the American courses in content. However, it was so badly presented, and so theoretical, that, after three or four weeks, three quarters of the participants had dropped out. Teaching adults had been my career. I was good at it. My degree was mainly psychology. I could see why the course I attended had been such a failure. People want practical ideas, something concrete which they can take home and put into operation, tools to help them make changes. So I wrote this book.

I feel a kind of bond with people who struggle through anxiety and depression. I have been through two depressions myself and so many of my friends are struggling with one or the other of these conditions. We avoid social events, worried that people will think badly of us, anxious that people will not like us, fearful that we might say the wrong thing, look stupid or not have anything interesting to say. We feel like the outsider looking in at a social, confident world where everyone seems happy and successful. And these negative thoughts about ourselves can keep us company all day and night.

So, now, I have learned to manage my thoughts better, and I have been passing on the principles of Mindfulness and Positive Thinking in these eight week courses, called Positive Living, for several years in several centres in central England. The level of success has been amazing. People's lives have changed for the better. This course really works. People have substantially reduced their negative thinking and have learned new techniques to help them do that. The book has evolved naturally from the course. Treat the book as your own course and give yourself a couple of months to work through it. Give yourself time to practise and get used to doing each exercise over and over again until it becomes a good habit replacing your old bad one. You will learn to control your thoughts, stop giving yourself a hard time, face the future with less fear and more confidence, connect yourself more with the outside world and focus more on the good things in your life.

The advice and medical evidence I use are borrowed from the NHS, the British Heart Foundation, the British Medical Association and other reputable sources. The exercises I suggest come from experts in the field, from Cognitive Behavioural Therapy including Mindfulness practices, from experts in Positive Psychology, from existing happiness courses and from experts in physical health. All I have done is translate them into plain English.

You might think about finding someone to follow this course with you. You'll have someone to discuss the ideas with and to keep you on track.

Covid-19 and Isolation

As you read this book, it will become clear just how important social interaction is for our physical and mental well-being if you didn't know that already. For many of us, prolonged isolation means prolonged loneliness. We are sometimes kept apart from friends, family and, in lockdown, even neighbours. And it is something we are just not used to and have had no training for. In this unfortunate situation, we are ripe for attacks of negative thinking. We feel powerless to do anything about our loneliness and our negative thoughts, and we can't get out to meet other people.

There are some ideas here which can help you to cope. Sometimes the loss of contact with people can feel like a bereavement. There is a temptation to sit down in your armchair, or stay in bed, and allow negativity to take you over. There are techniques in this book which may at least give you some respite from your negative thoughts.

Things people have said about this course

I feel I have got back control of my mind.

I am not everybody's dogsbody any more.

I have got more energy. I am getting things done.

I have started a ladies' social group. I am learning the ukulele. I spent Christmas working with the homeless at the Salvation Army. (This woman was 84.) I have rented a flat in Italy and I am going to learn Italian. (A retired woman) This was four people from the same group.

I am going to a meditation group.

I like myself more.

Last week, I realised what a waste of time negative thinking is. I have stopped doing it and my outlook has completely changed. (This is what a woman said to the group at the start of the second class.)

I am getting on better with people.

I have started to appreciate the good things in my life.

I am not as anxious as I used to be.

I can't believe how much pressure I used to put on myself.

I am much more organised now, and my kids are too.

I am better at saying no to people.

I know how to stop myself thinking negatively.

I used to lie in bed for an hour in the mornings thinking bad thoughts. Now I get up when I wake up and my day is much better.

I have stopped leaving my assignments till the last minute. (A university student.)

Chapter 1

Negative thinking 1

Bad habit: letting my brain lapse into negative thinking.

You're watching your favourite series on TV, reading a book, cleaning the car, digging the garden, even sitting with friends. Ten minutes in and your thoughts are wandering. Now you are thinking about some problem in the past, maybe having negative thoughts about yourself, or some issue at home or at work, or maybe your thoughts have gone to the future and your anxieties about what might happen next. But, hang on, you sat down to watch the TV, read a book etc. So why are you now thinking about something else? Who is in charge of your brain here?

This lapsing into negative thinking happens to millions of us.

Here's a story told to me not long ago about the husband of a woman in one of my classes.

He was on holiday in Spain with his family. The beach was beautiful, surrounded by palm trees, restaurants, bars and hotels, blue sky and sunshine. The sound of children's laughter was everywhere. The smells of food and suntan oil wafted by him. It sounds heavenly, doesn't it? Was he lying there appreciating all of these wonders and really enjoying himself? Sadly not. Some months before, he had lent some money to his brother and, since then, his brother had never mentioned it again even though he was earning reasonable money. He didn't want to risk asking his brother and maybe risk their friendship. So he bottled it up and swirled it round in his head day after day, night after night.

He was possibly thinking something like this:

"He's my brother, he should know better. I don't mind lending him money but if you say you're gonna pay it back, you pay it back. It's the principle of the thing. I am not rich. I can't throw money around. He said he'd pay me back in a month. I mean what am I? A mug? I'll never lend him money again. He hasn't even mentioned it. What am I supposed to do? If I ask him, he'll fall out with me and then I'll never get it back ………………………….." and so on and so on and so on, every day.

This poor man, who had selected this holiday, because he needed a break from his daily work-heavy life back home, had actually brought his problems with him to Spain along with his passport and his family.

Did his brother even know he was thinking this stuff?

Did these thoughts change anything?

Was he thinking the same thoughts over and over again?

How was it all making him feel? Happier or more miserable?

Many of us do this. This book is about taking back control of your mind and getting rid of this damaging way of thinking. Slowly, you will learn to take more control over your brain. Negative thinking is a bad habit we can break. We are going to tackle these automatic negative thoughts which can turn us into quite miserable people.

What are these negative thoughts we need to get away from?

If you are in the middle of something that is going on right now, a problem with someone, pressure, pain or bad news, maybe, you are entitled to give it all of your attention, to look for solutions, to feel negative and emotional. We are human after all. Life happens to us every day. Problems have to be dealt with. Some negative thoughts may be involved.

A lot of unhappy people, though, are spending their time recycling the same negative thoughts day after day, thoughts about the past or the future, negative thoughts about other people and themselves. The same thoughts may be looked at from a slightly different angle each day. Like the man on the beach, nothing changes except for the fact that this thinking will probably make you a little more miserable.

It is almost like we say to ourselves, 'Mmm, I am looking forward to this evening. My two favourite TV programmes are on. I'll make myself a nice cup of tea, settle into my favourite armchair, watch my programme for ten minutes and then I will allow myself to slip into some unpleasant thoughts. I'll remember that horrible thing my sister said last month, then I'll start to focus on all the mistakes I made as a parent and remind myself of the things I am not very good at, before deciding that all the plans I have got probably won't come to anything anyway. And then after an evening of gloom I will go to bed.'

Eckhart Tolle, one of the leading researchers in this field said, **"Your mind is an instrument, a tool. Thoughts are there to be used for a specific task, and when the task is completed, you lay them down. As it is, I would say about 80 to 90% of most people's thinking is not only repetitive and useless, but because of its dysfunctional and often negative nature, much of it is also harmful."**

So there it is, straight from the expert's mouth: much of our thinking is repetitive, negative, a waste of time and can be quite destructive. Thoughts pass through our heads all day long, thousands of them. Are we going to hold on to every one, especially the repeating negative ones? I like this following idea.

Treat thoughts as fizzy water or champagne bubbles

Let them just rise to the surface and disappear. If they are useful, of course, if they are about what you are doing at the moment, you hold on to them. But if they are of no consequence, or negative, or destructive, just let them go through your brain and out the other side.

So now we are beginning to get an idea of the target. We need to start to get to know our brains and what they do, and especially how they lead us up miserable paths. We need to recognise when, where and at what times we are prone to negative thoughts. And then we need to practise switching away from them. So before you go on to the next chapter, spend a few days noticing how your brain behaves, and when and where your thoughts get negative and which negative thoughts keep cropping up on a regular basis.

The woman who needed only one lesson

I run classes on this subject. A woman in one of my groups went home after the first class and began to realise she was angry all the time and had been for a couple of years. Her friend had even pointed it out to her. Her problem was that she had been betrayed by someone close and that was the cause of her anger. She told me that the part that made her realise what she was doing to herself was when I said everybody else was getting on with their own lives, and nobody in the world gave any thought to what was going on in her head. She came back the second week and said everything had changed. She had realised that this useless anger was ruining her life, and it was changing nothing, so she stopped doing it. The difference in her was amazing. (It is not usually as quick as that, but this is a true story.)

Homework

Get to know your brain and how it behaves. Notice when and where, or maybe with whom, you lapse into negative thinking. This is your first major test. Your attitude to this homework will set the tone for the whole programme. It is not a one-time homework. Ideally you will spend a lot of your time in the next few weeks thinking about what subjects you allow your mind to think about and when and where you slip into negative thinking. If you are serious about feeling better about yourself, it starts here.

Make a list of those negative thoughts which keep coming up in your mind. We are going to learn to control them. Notice, too, the times when you are NOT bothered by negative thoughts.

When you have done this homework for a few days and you are getting familiar with how, when and where your mind behaves negatively, move on to the next chapter. Don't rush this.

Chapter 2

Negative Thinking 2

Bad habit: worrying or thinking about things we can do nothing about.

In Chapter One, we agreed that negative thinking is bad for us. Your homework was to spend a few days noticing what happens to your thoughts and when, where, with whom and how often you are prone to slipping into negative thought.

As a result of doing this, a man in one of my groups realised that he spent the first half hour of each day lying in bed with a cup of tea, thinking negative thoughts, giving himself a hard time and worrying about things. So now, instead of lying there, he gets up when he wakes up and does something different. He says it has made an amazing difference to how he approaches the day ahead. He says he feels he has taken control of himself.

The opening of this book asked you if you got distracted and, maybe, slipped into negative thinking while you were watching TV, reading a book, cleaning the car etc. This is what happens to a lot of people. You decided to watch TV and you ended up thinking about things which make you miserable and which you probably think about repeatedly.

But your mind decided to watch TV and now it is doing something else.

Did you want that to happen? Did you choose to get dragged down into negative thought? I don't think so. Many of you might answer, 'It just happened. I had no control over it.' In Mindfulness literature, and in Cognitive Behavioural Psychology, this very common behaviour is known as Automatic Negative Thinking.

Automatic negative thinking is something we can change. We need to get to know our brains better and then start telling them what they are not allowed to do.

The secret to getting away from negative thinking is to have somewhere else you can go with your thoughts.

Years ago, I had a stop smoking book. It advised me to break my old habits. Don't sit in your favourite armchair where you like to smoke. Don't sit down after a meal because you like to smoke then. Do something else instead. Wash the dishes, go for a walk, sit in a different room. It's the same with stopping negative thinking. Get out of the armchair, change your activity. Do something else. Break your old ways. Remind yourself that it really is just a bad habit.

This book is going to give you lots of ideas for alternative things you can do. Choose the ones which work for you. Here are a couple of simple ideas to get you started. Stop what you are doing and give them a proper go. This is a good way to show you that you can control your thinking.

- Find a picture or photograph which you like and spend two minutes really studying it, the colours, expressions, lines, scenery, background etc. While you are doing this you will almost certainly find your thoughts wander off. That's normal: we are human beings. Just realise and accept what has happened, then bring your thoughts back to the picture. Don't give yourself a hard time: we all wobble when we start learning new things. *I remember one young woman saying, 'Wow, that was really relaxing'.*

- Using your hearing this time, choose a piece of music you like, preferably gentle music, just a few minutes long. Close your eyes and imagine that you and the music are the only two things in the world. Focus all of your attention onto the music, the sounds, the words, the instruments, the rhythm, the melody. Your thoughts will probably wander again. Just bring them back to the music without being hard on yourself for drifting off. It's normal.

You have just proved twice that you can control what you think about and which thoughts you want to focus on. If your thoughts strayed away from the picture or the music, you were, firstly, able to recognise that your thoughts had strayed and, secondly, you were able to switch your thoughts back to the thing you had decided to do. **So you can control your thoughts if you choose to**.

Some of you found these exercises hard. Some will say I just can't do it. And if you found it difficult, just remember that this is a new skill you are learning, an old habit you are breaking, so it won't be so easy at first, but the more you practise the better you get.

The thing is, if you do either or both of these two short exercises on a regular basis, you will have found a very simple way to declutter your brain and get rid of all the garbage in there. It doesn't have to be a photo every time: it can be anything you find interesting to look at, a view from your window, a flower in a vase, an ornament on your mantelpiece, the pattern of your curtains or wallpaper.

By focussing on these things, you are emptying your mind of everything else. That is why you are doing it. Have you ever had that feeling of being completely lost in a book, a piece of music, or a view where nothing else existed? That is the kind of place we are trying to get to for a few minutes whenever our thoughts are getting too much for us.

So how does this work?

You may think that just a couple of minutes is not long enough and that you will immediately return to your negative thoughts when your exercise has finished. But this is not the case. Somehow, you have reset your brain and it is able to let go of what you were thinking before, on most occasions. And the more you practise, the better you get.

Here's a story. (It doesn't apply to everyone.)

You and your friend sign up for a beginners' class at something, say, badminton. You notice that your friend is doing better than you are. Negative thoughts want to take you over. 'I am useless', 'I'll never be any good at anything', 'I can't do this,' 'I am always making mistakes', 'I can't get the hang of this', 'People will think I am stupid', 'She's better than me.'

But you are supposed to be listening to the teacher, practising and learning something new. That is your 'here and now'. That is what you signed up for. What's all this negative stuff? That's not what you chose to do. You came to learn something and now you are beating yourself up because it is difficult. Stay focussed on what you are doing. Tell all those other thoughts in your head to clear off (or maybe something stronger).

So where are these thoughts coming from? Have you held onto untrue things which your parents or your teachers or so-called friends said about you? Things like, 'You're useless, thick, a waste of space. You'll never make it', for example. Have you got used to this bad habit of having a downer on yourself? Are these thoughts doing you any good? Do you really want to let these other people's voices play around in your head and put you down? When you're learning something new, you are bound to make mistakes. If you can do it already, what's the point of signing up?

A lot of us post-war children, and many younger ones too, grew up with strict parents who found it difficult to say things like, 'I love you', or 'I am proud of you', or even, 'Well done'. And we spent a lot of time and effort trying to please these mute parents who found criticism easy and praise very difficult. And it left us with the feeling that we weren't very good at anything despite all the evidence to the contrary. And this negative thought stayed with us long after we had left home. Were these negative thoughts of ourselves true? No. Many of us became successful parents, with lots of friends, good at our jobs and skilled at sports, music or any other activities we pursued. But still inside us was a voice that told us all the bad things we were, and none of the good.

It is time to stop listening to those other voices. They are not yours. Kick them out.

Thoughts are not facts.

Treat these negative thoughts about yourself as bad ideas passing through your mind like bubbles. They are not true. Let them pass through. You don't want them. Many of us will have guiltily wished someone dead in our private thoughts. Does that make us murderers? No, we know it was just a passing thought and we dismissed it. You can learn to switch away from thoughts you don't want.

Let's go back to what Eckhart Tolle said in Chapter One. He reckons 80-90% of our thoughts are repetitive, useless and can be harmful. These are the thoughts we need to let go of. Thoughts are not facts. Just because you are thinking these bad thoughts about yourself doesn't mean they are true. Come on, look at all the good things you have done.

You receive a phone call, you see who it is, and you don't want to speak to them, so you don't answer. You had the choice, answer or don't answer. Can you do the same with your thoughts? I think so.

Can I learn to stop negative thoughts?

Yes! There are times when we find ourselves in a negative frame of mind. The first priority is to recognise what our brain is doing, particularly if it is thinking negatively. Then we need to have some techniques to switch away from negative thinking. Whatever we are doing we have the **choice** to stay focused on it or allow our minds to wander off. At the beginning of this course it is normal for our thoughts to wander. By the end, you will have much more control of your thinking and how your brain works. Learning how to focus on the things we are doing, and **choosing** not to hold onto other thoughts, means we are more likely to do our thing more efficiently, more quickly and more successfully. How often have you heard people say, 'He failed because he wasn't focussed', or 'She didn't have her mind on the job. She was somewhere else.'?

People in Japan have a saying, **'When you eat, eat. When you walk, walk.'**

Do one thing at a time, and think only of that one thing.

All these extra thoughts are a nuisance. They get in the way. Your body is here and your mind is somewhere else. Whose life are you living? Yours or somebody else's? Who decides what you think about? You or those other people's voices?

Just the other day, a lady in one of my groups told me she used to watch TV with her mobile phone and her tablet on her lap, and she switched between the three. Now she has abandoned the other stuff and focusses only on watching TV. **'When you watch TV, watch TV.'** Her brain is now only thinking about the TV programme. Her body and her mind are doing the same thing.

Eckhart Tolle again, on fear of the future and non-forgiveness of the past.

"Unease, anxiety, tension, stress, worry - **all forms of fear** - are caused by too much future and not enough presence. Guilt, regret, resentment, grievances, sadness, bitterness and **all forms of non-forgiveness** are caused by too much past and not enough presence."

Fear. Fear of things which haven't even happened yet. Fear which will change nothing in the future but will make you miserable now. Try to switch your thoughts to what is going on NOW. Try to get your mind away from the future.

Forgiving is hard. Some of us find it hard to forgive ourselves and some of us find it hard to forgive other people. We keep beating ourselves up about things we have done. And we hold grudges against other people. And we churn nasty thoughts about these other people which twist us up and make us bitter and angry. And what changes? Nothing.

You don't have to be best friends with someone after you have forgiven them. You haven't done it for them: you have done it for yourself. You've done it because you have had enough of these unpleasant thoughts swilling around in your brain. "Let it go, man." Easy to say but hard to do. But remember you are doing this to make yourself happier. You are getting anger and resentment out of your system.

Tolle's message is clear; get out of the future and the past and into the present i.e. think about what you are doing now.

Bereavement

A few people have arrived at my courses having lost someone close. Of course, we think negatively at these times. But grief is a process we need to go through and there are no rules, no set times, no magic pills or techniques which can stop you grieving or ease your pain. I used to work as a bereavement counsellor for CRUSE, a very useful and free support for people who have lost someone close. I learned that humans have an amazing ability to heal, to get stronger and to start living again.

The bereaved people who have visited my course have got to a point where they consider they are ready to start moving forward after a long period of grief. One thing which really helped them was being in a group and socialising again. They were able to talk and share and feel accepted. And they took from the course only what they needed. I have to say it was beautiful to watch people making that transition, to stop suffering alone.

Do you have trouble remembering things?

Do you struggle to remember details of conversations? When you listen, are you really listening? Or is your mind somewhere else? Is it hard to remember things you have read, dates, places and names, for example? Is it any wonder if you weren't completely there when you read them? Maybe half of your mind was thinking about some job you had to do, or what you were going to say to someone when you saw them, or a lie you needed to make up to explain some mistake you had made, or any one of a billion other possible thoughts. How can you expect to remember things if you weren't 100% there in the first place?

The secret to a better memory is to be completely focussed on what you are doing. Then you are more likely to remember. Keep yourself in the moment, the here and now. Let the other thoughts go. **When you listen, listen. When you read, read.**

Here and Now - two ways to relax and think only of one thing

From the first page of this chapter, you can see how important it is to focus on the thing you are doing now and not let other thoughts get in the way. Of course, if you have decided to sit down and plan your future, that is OK. You are planning. That is your 'here and now': that is what you **chose** to do. But there is a big difference between planning for the future and worrying repeatedly or being anxious about some future event.

Our body is with us all the time. Whatever we do, our body is there, always in the present, the here and now, the moment. So if we want to bring ourselves away from thoughts we don't want, and into the here and now, thinking about our body is a great way to start. Here are two more exercises which can bring us into the present.

Sit comfortably somewhere, upright with your bottom right in the back of your chair, your back straight and your head up, your feet flat on the floor and your hands in your lap. If your legs aren't long enough to reach the ground, put your feet on a cushion. Now start to be aware of your breathing. Try to follow your breath up through the nostrils, into the back of the throat and down your wind pipe. Feel your abdomen (your middle) rise and fall.

Are you breathing into your chest or your middle? Try to take your breath down so that it is your abdomen which moves in and out and not your chest. If you can't manage it, just take your breath into the lower part of your chest. Relaxed breathers breathe into the abdomen. Advanced breathers can even breathe into the lower part of their belly.

You can do this for a few minutes anywhere, at work, in the kitchen or your armchair. It is a great little exercise for getting you away from negative thoughts, for giving your body and brain a rest and for giving yourself a recharge.

That exercise and this one below can be done in a few minutes. They are useful ways of calming you down, relaxing you. This next exercise enables you to give your body a little check-up and to get rid of any physical and mental tension you may feel.

Keep the same sitting position as above and focus on your breathing, the in breath and the out breath. Keep them about the same length. Now, use the out breath to drain tension from your body.

Start with your face and your jaw muscles in particular. As you breathe out, allow the tension in your muscles to drain downwards through your jaw. Feel your jaw drop as your muscles relax on each out breath. Do it a few times.

Then move down to your neck and shoulders. Feel the tension draining down and out of your muscles on each out breath. You should feel your shoulders dropping a little. Some people report that their neck feels like it is getting a little longer.

Continue this process through the upper arms, the lower arms, fingers and hands. Feel the dead weight of your completely relaxed hands on your lap.

Take this same process down through your legs and become aware of the weight of your bottom on the chair and your feet on the floor.

Of course, it is relaxing to listen to music, study a photo, watch TV, or to think only of your breathing or your body. But the real value of these exercises is that suddenly your brain has the opportunity to think of only one simple thing. And while it is doing that small task, the rest of your brain is taking a very well-earned break. And, afterwards, it is more alert and ready to take on the next task. **Brain rest is essential if we are going to manage our hectic lives.** There is a chapter on brain rest later in the book.

You can find hundreds of relaxation exercises on the internet, YouTube, for example. These two exercises above aren't perfect for everybody. Google 'relaxation techniques' or 'relaxation music' and find one that works for you.

Do you have trouble getting off to sleep?

Try either or both of these exercises above when you go to bed. Empty your mind and let your body relax. The brain won't let you go to sleep if it is full of things which are bothering you, or if your body is tense. Bring your thoughts down to one simple thing, like breathing or relaxing your muscles, and bring those thoughts back when they wander off. Think about your middle rising and falling as you breathe. Or become aware of the feeling of air passing through your nostrils and into your throat. Perhaps you would prefer to think about your jaw, neck and shoulders relaxing as you breathe out.

This is my preferred method of getting off to sleep or getting back off to sleep in the middle of the night. I used to not remember to do the relaxation when I woke up at 4.00a.m, and I carried on thinking my negative thoughts, my worries and my memories. As the Mamas and Papas used to sing,'The darkest hour is just before dawn.' So, remembering to think of my breathing, especially when I woke up in the middle of the night, was something I had to get used to. It is a new habit. You don't learn it in one night. The more you do it, the easier and more natural it gets.

Homework

Practise any or all of the four exercises in this unit every day if you can. They only take a few minutes each and they can make you feel refreshed and ready to go.

Try to be aware of what you are doing here and now, in this particular moment, and bring your mind back to that thing when your thoughts wander.

There was a lot of new stuff in this chapter. You can't remember it all in one go. Give yourself a week or two to read it a few times, and practise the exercises and see which ones you like. This chapter is the big one. If you find yourself agreeing with what it says, all you have to do is make a firm decision to stick with it and do the work. Take a couple of weeks away from the book now. Start to practise these exercises. Get to know to what your mind does, how it behaves and how it does its own thing if you let it.

Chapter 3

Are you struggling with this?

My own struggle

I may sound like a bit of a 'know all' telling everybody what to do and making it sound so easy. But, believe me, I know how hard it is, especially at the beginning before you have made much progress. In the introduction to this book, I described my own struggles with negative thinking fifteen years ago. These changes in our thinking, especially switching away from negative thinking, are new skills we have to learn. It is not easy to keep yourself at it.

The first struggle was to even realise I was thinking negatively. Then a bell would ring in my head. "Tim, you are doing it. Pack it in." Then I would start trying to switch my thoughts to other subjects, getting out of my armchair, doing a relaxation exercise, going for a walk, calling a friend or thinking of the good things in my life. And, as the weeks went by, I got quicker at recognising that I was thinking negatively and became much better at switching my thoughts away. I kept reminding myself that these thoughts were harmful and did me no good at all. So why would I put up with them?

You can do it too. Don't give up on yourself. You **can** stop your negative thinking.

Take your mind back to when you bought this book. Remind yourself why you bought it. Life wasn't a bunch of roses and you needed something to help you change things. You also probably knew that you couldn't make changes just by flicking your fingers. Some work and effort would be needed. But then life got in the way, like it was pulling you back to the place you were trying to get away from. So this chapter is just a little nudge for you to remind you of your desire to make your life more satisfying. This book does make demands on you but you can handle them quite easily if you just stick at it. So, if you are struggling to stay with it, just read the rest of this section, tell yourself that you can do it and start the book again if you need to.

In Negative Thinking 1, for your homework, I asked you to pay some attention to how your brain behaves and, particularly, when and where you might find yourself slipping into repeated negative thinking. Getting to know yourself and the way your mind works will be useful in identifying problems and making plans to solve them. If you are determined to change and get away from negative thoughts, this work is essential. You just have to say to yourself,' I am gonna do it'. Write it on your wall or in your diary or on your phone calendar. Better still ask a friend to do it with you.

In Negative Thinking 2, I suggested some techniques for switching away from negative thinking. These are not easy to learn, especially at the beginning and you have to keep on practising to get better. Here is what some people report. They say they realised they were thinking negatively, so they used the exercises to try and switch to something more positive. But it was a struggle at first. Picture the badminton beginner. Practice makes perfect. You can't learn anything worthwhile without making a few mistakes and maybe having a little self-doubt.

It has to be that way with your negative thinking too. It's a bad habit you have had for a long time. You can't change overnight. Accept it that negative thoughts will keep poking their noses in. You are a beginner learning a new skill. Stick at it, and you will be rewarded. Take yourself back to your breathing and/or body scan and try again. Or, change what you are doing. Move somewhere else. Get away from the place where you like to think negatively. At first, it may be only a few seconds that you can do it, but, slowly, the more you practise, the easier and more natural it becomes, and the longer you are able to replace your negative thoughts with more positive ones. And gradually you start to feel successful as you begin to realise that **you** are in control of your brain and not those gremlins which sneak in and take you over.

This can be your crutch to lean on, your support when things aren't going well, your way to take back control of yourself. Everybody who has completed my eight week course has said their life has improved. They have some tools to help them through difficult times. No tricks, no gimmicks, just common sense, i.e. negative thinking is damaging, so I am going to learn how to stop. It's not much different from smoking, really, another bad habit that is hard to stop, but is worth the struggle.

Chapter 4

Me Time

Bad habit. I put me at the bottom of my list.

Imagine you were a car and you saw another car in trouble. And you discover that a part from your engine will solve their problem, a filter maybe. So you give them your filter. But now you are spluttering along the road.....and nobody is offering you their filter.

Are you one of those people who does all the giving, who believes that other people's needs are more important than your own? A lot of older people, and some younger ones too, definitely have that feeling. They grew up being told, 'Other people are more important than you are. It is selfish to think about yourself'. But hang on, how come everybody else gets to do their own thing sometimes, and we don't? What's wrong with a bit of selfishness sometimes? It only means putting yourself first. Some of us have got the idea that we were put on the planet to solve everyone else's problems. Everyone else is important, and worth looking after, but we don't seem to be. How does that make you feel?

Or, maybe you're one of those people who works all hours God sends? Evenings and weekends, you're either working or exhausted. No time or energy to put yourself first and do what you want to do. In her excellent book, 'The Top Five Regrets of the Dying', Bronnie Ware listed this regret as No. 2:

"I wish I hadn't worked so hard."

She said every male she listened to expressed this regret. (Most of the old women she talked to hadn't been bread winners in their earlier days, but some did list this regret.) And the men regretted that they had missed their children growing up. Bronnie Ware worked with hundreds of terminally ill, mostly old, people. The title of her book may sound a bit morbid, but, actually, old people are wise and their experiences can teach us a lot. They listed this next one as their biggest regret of all:

"I wish I had had the courage to live a life true to myself, not the life others expected of me. Dreams I have had have gone unfulfilled due to the choices I made."

What a thing to say at the end of your life. 'I didn't fulfil my dreams.' 'I didn't do what I wanted to do'. 'I spent my life trying to live up to other people's expectations.' You can get to the end of your life and say, 'Hang on, where did that go? There were so many things I wanted to do but I never put myself first. I was too busy looking after everybody else'

That word **'courage'** is in there too. It does take some courage to give up your old bad, but familiar, habits and let the world know you are going to change.

'Me time' is the chance for you to be yourself, to exercise your own individuality, to be that character who is different from everyone else. This is the time when you are not a worker, a student, a housekeeper or a parent, but a free person who can make your own choices, indulge in your own tastes, improve your own skills and follow up your interests or passions. This is the time when you have no obligations to anyone else.

A friend of mine was seeing a counsellor some years ago to get help with his depression. The counsellor asked him to describe his day. (My friend was a teacher.)

"Well, I get up at 6.30, have a quick breakfast and I am out by 7. I walk to school: it takes about half an hour. I go straight to my classroom and spend the next hour preparing for the day. Then the children arrive. After school, I often run a sports club or rehearsals for the school play and, if not, I will work after school before walking home at about 5pm. I pick up a ready meal at Tesco on the way and then I get down to some planning *and marking ready for the next day at school. I go to bed about 10pm."*

The counsellor replied, "Am I supposed to be impressed?"

My friend was instantly shocked, but the message hit home fairly quickly. He had felt proud to say how dedicated he was to his work. But the counsellor was keen to explain that Jack was living like a slave to other people's needs. He had no 'me time', no time for his own needs and interests, no time for a long soak in the bath, or a walk in the local park, or an evening with friends, the cinema, a girlfriend even. He had no 'me time', no time to be himself, despite living alone. It is not surprising he was going through depression.

So, how do I make myself some 'me time'?

Be selfish: put yourself first sometimes.

I can hear you saying, 'That's easier said than done', and you are right. But we are not asking you to abandon other people, just put yourself on the list of people who need your attention and make some time for you.

How about making your own timetable and getting others to fit into your gaps occasionally?

How to get started

If you are living with or very close to other people, they will need to know about your changes, otherwise you will end up fitting into their gaps again. If you want to change your life significantly, it makes sense that people close to you know what you want, and they fit around you for a change. Otherwise you will be sneaking around again fitting into other people's gaps.

So, **No.1** is to tell people close to you that you need some 'me time'. Tell them at certain times you will be busy and not available. You may want to put a timetable on the kitchen door, or some other visual reminder, letting people know when your 'me time' is. If you are not an assertive person, you may find it difficult to say no to people. Having your plans there for everyone to see could make that a little easier for you. If you have children, they can get used to this, too, and give you some space.

Here are just a few ideas for creating some 'me time'.

- Delegate some of your jobs to other people, housemates, members of your family. (If you can afford it, pay a cleaner.)

- If you have children, get together with some friends and sort out a babysitting circle. You send your kids to them once a week and you have theirs another night. Maybe you could make it a regular night out with a friend or a partner.

- Have a look at all of the things you do and ask if they are really necessary. I knew a woman who vacuum cleaned her living room four times a day, every day. Is everything **you** do really necessary?

- Try to decide what things you are really interested in and start reading about them in books or on the internet. Just get the ball rolling.

- Go food shopping once or twice a week instead of five or six. Or order your food online.

- Put strict limits on your social media time.

What to do with your 'me time'.

One of the main functions of 'me time' is to give yourself a chance to step away from your daily chores, to switch your mind off from all of the things you have got to do. How do **you** relax? What do **you** like to do? Sometimes it can be almost nothing, while others enjoy studying, going out, playing, inviting friends etc. Remember that while you are doing these things the rest of your brain gets a chance to take a break provided that you don't slip into negative thoughts or start worrying what you **should** be doing. Stay in the moment. Think only about what you are doing.

If you google 'Me time', just as with many of the subjects in this book, you will find a thousand ideas for things to do. Different ideas will suit different people. See what works for you. I have listed a few below.

Think about inviting someone to do some of these things with you.

- Stay away from negative people if you can.

- Invite someone to play a board game or cards.

- Go swimming, shopping, walking, jogging or go out for a drink.

- Do some reading, painting pictures, painting and decorating, colouring in (there are some great colouring books for adults), listen to some music, pot some plants, sow some seeds.

- Take a long bath, a stroll, a brisk walk, a trip to a place of interest to you. But always keep your mind in the present.

- Meditate. See next chapter.

- Go on the internet, or to the library, and follow up something you're interested in, like flowers, trees, birds, famous people, history, celebrities, sports heroes.

- Play some songs you like on Youtube and sit down and really listen to them, or dance to them. Try a new recipe, join a cookery class, join a local club. Volunteer for something you are interested in. Your local library will have a notice board with these kinds of opportunities.

- Join an interest group or sign up for a class and learn something new. Your local schools, colleges and community centres have free and paying courses.

There are local magazines which come through the door which contain information in the back pages about local social group meetings, choirs, cookery, gardening, walking, Rotary Clubs, Lions clubs, crafts, meditation, local history. YourCall is a useful magazine often available in libraries and community centres.

There is no limit to this section. These are just a few ideas.

Remember that learning is great for our brains. Use it or lose it, older people especially.

Remember that exercise is good for our bodies and brains.

Remember that social interaction can make us live longer and healthier.

Should, Ought, Must

We say these words to ourselves a lot. Other people say them to us when they are giving us advice.

I should/ought/must call so and so.

You should tell him to mind his own business.

I must start learning to sew.

I ought to lose some weight.

Where is this rule book that tells you all the things you **should** be doing? Why can't you be yourself and do what you **want** to do? Usually, if someone tells you

you **should** be doing something, they are telling you what they would do in the same position. But you are you and they are not you. Be yourself. Then you won't get to the end of your life with regret that your dreams were unfulfilled.

"Be yourself: everybody else is taken." (Oscar Wilde)

You can't be anyone else. Let it go.

Homework

Decide what you want to do with your new 'me time'. How do you like to relax? What are you interested in? What have you always wanted to have a go at? Your mind and body need breaks from the pressures of everyday life. How are you going to do that? How do you enjoy yourself?

Once you have chosen your activities, decide when you want to do them, then let those around you know that this is going to be your time. Do some research to find out where you can do these things. You have a right to take some time off and to look after yourself. It is not just a right: you actually need it. Your batteries need recharging on a regular basis. Do yourself a favour and put yourself first for a change.

Chapter 5

Brain Rest

Bad habit: we rest our bodies but not our brains.

This book is largely about common sense. We have learned all kinds of bad habits, and we get so used to them we don't realise we've got them. We'd like to feel more relaxed, have some control, have some time to ourselves, be more organised, sleep better, have a better memory, spend time with friends, have some fun. But instead we find ourselves saying things like: "I can't do it: it is all too much. I can't cope. I can't remember things. I never seem to be able to get on top of life, to finish a job I started. **Life seems to be running away with me. I need a break. HEEEELP!"**

Let's have a look at how well we treat ourselves. Let's compare how well we take care of our cars, our bodies and our brains.

Your Car

You top it up so it always has the right amount of water, enough oil to keep it running smoothly, air in the tyres, and fuel, exactly the right kind to make sure it performs at its best. You get regular services to get the levels of clutch and brake fluid checked, change filters, plugs sometimes, and get old oil replaced. And on top of that you take it for an MOT every year to make sure it is safe, healthy (low emissions) and roadworthy. You want your car to be performing at its best, at its most efficient, so you take very good care of it.

Your Body

Are you taking in exactly the right kind and right amount of fuel (food, water, sunshine)? Is your body performing at its best? When your body isn't operating properly, do you immediately take it somewhere to get it fixed? Do you give your body regular check-ups? Do you take your body out for exercise on a regular basis to keep your battery charged?

Do you look after your body's filters, your lungs, your liver, your stomach, your skin, kidneys and intestines? **Do you take as much care of your body as you do your car?**

Your Brain

The brain controls everything we do, think and feel, as well as the automatic things we do like breathing, digesting etc. Sometimes we decide to look after our bodies by stopping smoking, cutting down alcohol, eating less fat, salt or sugar or doing some exercise. **When do we ever decide that we must look after our brains, give them a rest and pamper them?** Truthfully, most of us never think about our brain health at all: we just expect our brains to carry on regardless.

In these modern technological times our brains are subjected to almost unbearable pressures. Throughout all of our waking hours they are bombarded by anxiety, memories, emotional ups and downs, demands from our families, work, friends, even from ourselves, bills, rent, mortgages, deadlines, targets, the next meal, expectations, promises, noise, computers, telephones, television, traffic, children, safety, cooking, cleaning, buying things, responsibilities, obligations, family break up, death, illness, loss, advertisements, fashion, money, keeping up with the Jones's, desires, relationships with all kinds of people and a million other things too.

So I will ask again, when do you say, 'Mmm, my brain is overloaded: I am going to give it a rest?' OK, we sleep, but often not well enough these days. Is it any wonder that talk of stress, anxiety and depression is commonplace?

So, how do I give my brain a rest?

This brain overload is normal life for most of us. And our brains have to process many of these thoughts at the same time. When do they get a break? And the unfortunate answer is that most of us never even think about giving our brains a rest. It is this intense activity which causes our brains to be tired, to not function well, to forget things, to come up with wrong answers, to make mistakes, to get confused, moody, angry and to get stressed. These kinds of difficulties are a breeding ground for negativity.

In Chapter 2 we looked at four ways of switching off, of thinking about only one thing. This is the basis of meditation which has been found to have seriously good effects on the brain. We shall look at meditation in detail later in this unit. We will learn how to sit down and switch our minds off.

How to switch off when you are busy.

In Chapter 2, we suggested that you think only about the thing you are doing e.g., shopping, watching TV etc. So, for example, when you are walking to the shop, you are only walking to the shop. You didn't choose to be brooding about your own or even other people's problems. You have decided you are walking to the shop. That is what you chose to do. And that walk involves your body and how you walk, the weather, the houses or fields that you pass, the sights, sounds and smells which surround you, etc. This is a chance to rest your brain. These things are your here and now. So, concentrate on them. Only them. And the simpler your thoughts are, the more rest your brain is getting.

Yeah but, no but, yeah but, how do you think about walking to the shops?

- First of all, your body. How are you walking? Are you upright and is your chin up; is your heel touching the ground first, and are your shoulders back? How we walk tells other people how we are feeling. Negative thinking people are more likely to be leaning forward, head down, rounded shoulders and walking slowly, lost in their own negative thoughts. Positive, confident people are more likely to be heads up, chests out, straight backed and taking in the world around them. So, think about how you are walking and how you look to other people.

- Maybe you are walking past houses, gardens, cars, trees etc. Notice them, the colours, the ones that need a lick of paint, the flowers in the gardens, the cracks in the pavement. What sounds can you hear? What smells do you notice?

- My mum used to sing out loud when she walked. We were embarrassed as kids but Mum was thinking of only one thing, the song she was singing.

What's the point?

- Number 1, your brain is getting a great rest while it is only having to think about one simple thing. It is recharging.

- You are not experiencing any strong emotions about the past, present or future. So that side of your brain is getting a rest too.

I know I repeat myself a lot in this book. But this message is very important and very simple. We overwork our brains in this modern hectic life we live, so that they just can't cope with everything that is thrown at them. They need breaks. And for those of you who will say, 'I feel a bit stupid looking at trees and pavement cracks', remember that nobody else knows what you are doing. And all you are doing is resting your brain.

When you eat, eat. Think only about your eating, the tastes, textures, smells, colours and temperatures of the food. And if your mind starts to wander into negativity, tell yourself, 'No', or 'Stop', and bring your mind back to the food. This is how you change bad thinking habits. Be aware of what your brain is doing and start to control it. You know it makes sense. When you are watching TV, ask yourself are you really watching it or are you allowing your mind to go where it wants to go?

Another very useful way to switch away from negativity, and rest your brain, is to keep a little store of good memories where you can take your thoughts while you are walking, washing the dishes, sweeping the floor, cleaning the car, travelling on a bus etc. When I find myself slipping into the negative, I conjure up pictures of my children when they were young. So, try to identify two or three good memories you have which you can call on when you realise you are thinking negative thoughts.

I got two speeding tickets within two weeks of each other. I asked myself why and realised that, when I was driving, I was NOT thinking about driving and especially not my speed. My mind was elsewhere. So now, when I drive, I drive. I look at the speedometer much more often, especially around town, and I haven't had a ticket in seven years. And no more negative thinking in the car.

Play

When did you last find yourself playing?

Why do children play and adults don't?

Do you enjoy playing?

Why don't you play any more?

Play can be physical and/or mental, from my grandson chasing me around the garden with a hosepipe, to sitting quietly around a card table playing rummy, or knockout whist.

What is play?

It is a special area of our lives, a place where we can go which leaves behind all the stresses of everyday life. Sometimes we need special equipment, like a hosepipe or a pack of cards, a table, a board game or a football. Usually we go to a different (or special) place to play, a room, swimming pool or the countryside, for example. Sometimes there is special clothing to wear like a swimsuit or trainers. We are making a decision to transfer, to move to a different place which has special rules and behaviours which we must follow, and this special, safe place takes us away from daily life and stress.

I remember having trouble persuading a friend of mine to come and play badminton. After the session, he said, 'I am so glad you pushed me to play. I feel great.' That 'I feel great' feeling came from a few sources: the pleasure hormones serotonin, dopamine and norepinephrine which are stimulated by exercise, the relaxation he felt after he had given his brain a rest, the satisfaction he felt for having exercised his body, and, maybe, the feeling of success he got from beating me. He was not thinking about his mortgage, his job, or the friend he had fallen out with. Sure, you have to concentrate when playing cards or badminton, but you are only concentrating on a relatively small and unimportant thing. **Caution: if you are a bad loser, find a non-competitive way to play, e.g listen to some music, walk the canal, dig the garden, read a book, try painting or get an adult colouring in book, or some other skill like sewing, quilting, cooking, learning a musical instrument.**

Yes, all of these activities can be described as play because they are removed from your everyday life. Your mind has been released. You are in the play area of your life. That is all you are thinking about.

When you are totally absorbed in your play activity, this is a kind of meditation. You have freed your mind from all of the worries, pressures, problems and anxieties which plague it on a daily basis. It is another reason why we feel so good after play. Our brains have taken a rest from all that daily hassle.

Meditation

There are so many views of meditation, so many images that come to mind. For many older people, it was unheard of until the Beatles told the world they were meditating and we associated meditation with long hair and bearded Indian religious people, always men. These days there is a much wider acceptance of the value of meditation for ordinary people like you and me. And we understand now that it is more than just a weird old hippie thing.

I first became interested when a friend of mine many years ago told me that he meditated before he went out for a late night. He said his energy lasted much longer and he felt calm all evening. I liked the sound of it; it worked for me too, and I went on to explore meditation more seriously. But I often go back to that conversation. He used meditation not for religious or spiritual reasons but just to refuel himself.

That is the kind of meditation I want to introduce in this book. You can move on to a deeper level at a later stage if you choose to. Find yourself a quiet place for ten or fifteen minutes every day and empty your mind, get rid of all the garbage in it. As a result, you will start to feel calmer and you will get more things done too. Science has actually shown that meditation changes your brain waves and makes you feel calmer. (Or is it 'karma'? ha ha)

Benefits of meditation. If you google this, 'benefits of meditation', you can draw your own conclusions but many researchers agree that meditation can reduce stress, make you calmer, lower blood pressure, improve sleep, memory and concentration. And it's free and you can do it anywhere.

How do I meditate?

I know some of you will have some funny ideas about meditation. Try to let them go. All you are doing is sitting there with your eyes closed, somewhere private, almost the same as if you were taking an afternoon nap. You are not in some kind of trance. You are just taking a break. Some of you will notice that your breathing gets more and more shallow the longer you meditate which is a sure sign that you are resting. If you want further proof, check your pulse rate before and after your session

There are many kinds of meditation. The one I describe here is the most popular and the most widely researched. If you google 'types of meditation', you will find that healthline.com will give you a good description of other types. But this method is simple, popular, well-researched and effective. (For other types of meditation there are lots of pieces of gentle meditation music on YouTube, or the sound of waves, birds or whales, for example, which you can use for ten minutes.)

- Find a comfortable chair in which you can sit upright with your bottom right up to the back of the chair. Put a thin cushion in your lower back to help you sit up straight if necessary. Or maybe sit on the cushion. You don't want to slouch.

- Keep your chin up. Try not to let your head flop forward.

- Have your feet flat on the floor and your hands in your lap.

- You might want to go into one of the breathing and relaxation exercises in Chapter 2, with your eyes closed, for a couple of minutes, just to get you in the right frame of mind.

- Before you start meditating, decide what you want your brain to do. Remember we are trying to get it to think of just one simple thing. Some people like to repeat a number in their head. Others have a special word, ideally a meaningless word or number that doesn't remind you of anything. Make up your own meaningless word, something that sounds soft and use it every time you meditate. Make it your personal word. I often just go to my word for a couple of minutes when I am stressed. Just thinking of the word takes me to a calmer place. I have put a list of words at the end of this section if you need any ideas.

- The secret is not to really concentrate hard on this word, the number or the music but just to allow it to be in your head, or even in your chest or your stomach. Just be aware that it is there without trying too hard to focus on it. And when your thoughts stray away, just notice what you have done and bring yourself gently back.

- Remember, this is a skill, and you are not going to master it first time. Everybody's thoughts stray at the beginning. Don't beat yourself up: just bring your awareness back to your word and continue. Start with ten minute sessions and slowly build them up as you get better at it. If you hear traffic noise or children playing, for example, just accept it, you can't change it, and bring your attention back to your word.

- You can keep a watch or quiet clock nearby and glance at it to keep your eye on the time. You are not in any kind of trance. If you have a few minutes left, just close your eyes and go back peacefully to your word or number. After a while you will not need the clock: you will know what ten or twenty minutes feels like.

- When your time is up just give yourself an extra minute or two to bring yourself very slowly back into the room before you open your eyes.

- Ten minutes every day is good, twenty is great. Try not to do it just after eating. A noisy stomach can distract you.

- Sometimes my groups can have quite lively or intense discussions. Then we do a ten minute meditation and when we emerge from it, everyone's voice is quieter, and there is a real atmosphere of peace in the room. Go on, treat yourself. Do some meditation.

Here are some ideas for your word but, by all means, make up your own:
kana, sharma, raya, yama, sema, tija, naja, binka, mura, hana, sira, chura, hanta, mesta

rayu, prindi, seru, hantu, manza, yaltu, geema, penti, forli,

turi, alsa, redon, simbon, shimun, karnia.

Any shortish meaningless word will do

Let this word be a very personal thing for you. Don't share it with anyone. After you have practised meditation for a couple of weeks, that word becomes associated with a peaceful, calm feeling. Sometimes, in daily life, when you are feeling stressed, just a minute or two with the word can calm you down considerably. It is another tool you can use to manage your negative thinking and enable you to switch your thoughts.

If this type of meditation doesn't work for you, or you feel you would like to be led through your meditation, google or YouTube , 'free guided meditation' and take your pick.

Homework

Think about the value of your brain. Ask yourself how you treat it. Be aware of how many things are going on inside there at the same time. Decide on your preferred ways to give your brain a rest. Do them.

Build some play into your life.

Practise meditation on a daily basis if you can; do it at a set time (part of your me time). Make a habit of it.

Chapter 6

Gratitude/Appreciation

Bad habit: not appreciating the good things in our lives.

Are you going to spend your spare time appreciating the good things in your life or moaning about the bad things, thinking about people you like or people you dislike? Which one is better for you?

Appreciating what you have got, or what or who is around you, is one of the basics of positive psychology. I can hear some of you saying, 'What have I got to be grateful for?' In some people's lives, the bad things are so powerful it is difficult to see beyond them. But most of us have a good side to our lives, things to be grateful for, but we just don't make the effort to appreciate the good bits.

Research has shown that people who practise gratitude on a regular basis

- **Are happier**

- **Visit the doctor less**

- **Are more generous**

- **More optimistic**

- **More likely to achieve their goals**

- **Have stronger immune systems**

- **Feel more alive with more positive emotions**

- **Sleep better**

- **Show more kindness and compassion**

Hang on, what did I just read? This is not a bad list. Have another look. If I could tick all these boxes, I'd be in a pretty good place. This gratitude business has some amazing effects. But we already know this. When we are positive, we feel better, we get more stuff done, and we are nicer to other people. And we get positive by thinking about the good things in our lives rather than being dragged down by the bad things. But some of us are prone to thinking only about the negative stuff. At bedtime, switch your thoughts to things that have gone well today, things you have appreciated. These can replace the more troubled thoughts you might have had, and the research says you will sleep better.

As I am writing this, the Covid-19 pandemic is with us, and we are confined to our homes. It isn't what we would choose. We have two main ways of looking at the situation, chin up or chin down. And one way to get your chin up is to say, 'What am I grateful for today?' 'What good things have happened?' 'What is good in my life?' An American friend, who lives alone, just told me she is glad (grateful) of the opportunity to clear a load of junk out of her apartment. She is not going to mope. Others have said they are writing and speaking to friends more than before. Lots of us are catching up on things we have been meaning to do for ages like painting the spare room or tending the garden. These are positive things, opportunities which we can either appreciate or just take for granted. I remember painting our spare room, and, for days afterwards, popping upstairs to have another look at it and feeling really pleased with what I had done. I had been meaning to do it for ages.

Let's get real

When you are in the middle of some bad event, the last things you want to start thinking about are the good things in your life. This bad business needs to be dealt with first. Somebody who has just been mugged, or had a flaming row with someone, or who has just learned she failed an exam, is not likely to want to start thinking about how lucky she is. You could strangle these people who say things like, "Cheer up, forget about it, let it go, man, always look on the bright side of life, pull yourself together."

But, if you go back a few chapters, you will recall that quite often we are thinking negatively even when nothing immediately bad is happening. And we can think like this wherever we are and whatever we are doing. And it is at these times that we have choices. First, we have to recognise that we are thinking negatively and then we need some positive thoughts to switch to. **Gratitude practice is an excellent place to go to for positive thoughts** if you want to stop routine, repetitive negative thinking.

Gratitude practice involves showing appreciation for all of the good things in our lives, things which we have in ourselves like health, determination, sense of humour, love, skills, experience, for example, and things which come to us from outside, from strangers, friends, family, the economy, nature, schools, hospitals, housing, employers,or maybe, holidays.

You might like to call it appreciation rather than gratitude. We are feeling gratitude when we start sentences with phrases like:

- **I love** ......

- **I'm glad that** ......

- **I feel lucky that** ......

- **I thank God that** ......

- **I appreciate** ......

- **I'm fortunate that** ......

- **That's nice** ......

- **Thank goodness** ......

- **This is brilliant**

So how do I practise gratitude?

It is easy to read books like this and say 'Mmm, that's a good idea, I must try it out', but you know you possibly won't get round to it. So you know it would be good for you, but you don't get round to doing it. As an example, I know a few people who think meditation is fantastic and makes them feel great. But they don't do it much. It is the same with keeping fit.

Like all of the exercises in these self help books, they all depend on you making a decision and sticking to it, for example, "From now on I am going to stop my negative thinking. I am going to notice when I do it and I am going to change my thoughts.' Later in the book, you are advised to make a list of all the things you have been putting off. You can either say you'll do it tomorrow or immediately find a pen and paper and start your list. Which of these two is you? It's about taking concrete steps not just casually promising yourself.

So, gratitude starts when you wake up in the morning. " I can get out of bed. Millions can't. I have a toothbrush, toothpaste, warm water, electricity, breakfast. Millions don't."

I was lucky to be born here in UK. I had no choice where I popped out. It could have been Syria, Yemen or Somalia. Thank goodness I wasn't born in those places.

War, famine, cholera. You see these poor people on the news. It could have been me ....or you. We had no choice where we were born. We dropped lucky.

Count up the whole range of things your body can do: see, hear, walk, eat, speak, play with your laptop or phone, play games, sports, work, smell, taste, feel. You are fortunate: millions are not, they can't do some of these things which we take for granted

Think about the good parts of your health, your friends, your family, colleagues, your home, your brain, your character. It isn't all bad is it? Think about what is going well in your life. Start off by remembering just a few of these things and have them ready for when you start feeling negative. It's your choice. **Positive or negative? Good thoughts or bad ones? Happiness or misery? Glass half full or half empty?** Decide to reprogramme yourself. Good thoughts about yourself, and about life in general, make you happy, and bad ones make you miserable.

Once your gratitude snowball starts rolling, it gets bigger and bigger. You start to feel more positive, so you appreciate more and more. It becomes a self-perpetuating good habit. You start to notice and remember the good things that are around you or in you. But you are the only one who can get it rolling. You have to make the change. Make a start. The longest journey starts with the first step.

A couple of ideas to help

It is good to think gratitude, but thoughts can disappear, so quite a few psychologists recommend that you do something a little more concrete like **writing things down.** Some suggest you write five positive things that have happened today. Find a time of day when you can do this on a regular basis, e.g. bedtime or after dinner. Some suggest that when you find yourself appreciating something good that has happened that you write it down and put it in a box, **a gratitude box,** full of notes about things for which you have felt grateful. Things you have achieved, skills and qualities that you have got, good things that other people have done for you, good things nature gives us like rain, sun, snow, a drying wind on washing day, a beautiful view, flowers, trees, birds, good things you own like a car, a phone or a TV. Remind yourself that there are billions of people in the world who don't experience these things, but you do. Open the box every so often and remind yourself of what's good in your life.

These ideas won't suit all of you, so find ones that work for you and practise them on a regular basis. Make them a good habit.

Here's a thing. A lot of people find that after a few days they are wanting to write down the same old things like 'I have got my health, a nice family, a job, nice house or car, maybe. I have nice holidays; my kids are healthy.' It's true. But if you are not prepared to dig deeper, you will write the same things down every day. So, men, for example, you could say 'I love my wife and I am lucky to have her', or you could break it down into smaller chunks, and just write or remember one of them a day e.g.

- She is decisive

- She's a great mum to our kids,

- She always asks how my day has been

- She makes me laugh

- She gets on great with my parents

- She comes up with good ideas for the family to do together

- She holds down a tough job

And next time you have a row, maybe you can go to these thoughts, after your angry period, to remind you what a great wife she is. Do the same with family, friends, workmates, neighbours, health, work, etc. You can do the same for all the different areas of your life. Break them down into smaller pieces. Why is X your best friend? Which parts of your body work well? What good things happen at work? What do you like about your car, your house, your phone, your football team or your man's cooking?

You could do the same for your last holiday, and remember the nice people you met, the food, the beach, the adventures. Or the kind things people have done for you today at work like bringing you a coffee, taking a message, offering you a cigarette, a biscuit, some help with something you were struggling with or asking after your family. Maybe somebody let you jump the queue at Aldi because you had only bought two things. These are the fizzy bubbles which we want to hold onto while we let the bad ones disappear into thin air.

None of these things is going to change your life on their own. Noticing them and remembering them, instead of just letting them pass you by, starts to put you in a more positive frame of mind and helps to remind you of the good in people. This is the start of your snowball. **So make a mental note, and keep it, when something good happens to you.** And gradually you will start to find yourself actually looking for the positive things in your day and remembering them.

What are your strengths?

People who feel low tend to focus their thoughts on their weaknesses. "I can't do this, I am no good at that. I wish I could………." Yet even though we are low, we still have positives, but we just dismiss them: we are still good at some things and we still have character strengths just like everybody else. It is not easy giving yourself credit when your spirits are down.

Try this kind of thinking. 'I am kind, I listen to people, I work hard, I am honest, I forgive people, I work well in a team, I make people laugh, I am loyal and hardworking, I am friendly, I am a good dad, mum, brother cousin, friend, son daughter, grandparent, I have had some successes this week. I am grateful for all these things.' **Make your own list. Remember these good things about yourself and appreciate them.** There is more on this subject in Chapter 8.

Compliments

To make gratitude work even better, why not tell your friends and relatives the things you like about them. We all love a compliment, and compliments have a habit of coming back to you. Mark Twain, the man who wrote Huckleberry Finn, said, 'A compliment will last me two weeks.' You have the power to improve somebody's life for two weeks just by saying something nice to them. I can remember the compliments I had as an adult. In the small groups I work with, people get to know each other quite well over eight weeks and, towards the end of the courses, compliments start to fly around the groups. And you can see the delight on the receivers' faces. A compliment is a lovely gift to someone. And they tend to come back to you, too. Compliment your children. That puts the cement between their bricks.

Health

Some of you reading this will be suffering ill-health. It is sometimes hard to see beyond the particular illnesses we have and actually list some of the good aspects of your health, e.g. your eyesight, hearing, healthy knees, no arthritis or kidney trouble or many other illnesses. A friend said to me once, 'Stop complaining about your knees. You should be grateful that they have lasted this long.' She was right. I don't complain any more. I have eyesight, hearing, two arms and legs, I can speak and smell things. I haven't got piles or varicose veins, heart disease, eczema or psoriasis, asthma, motor neurone disease, small head syndrome, or a million other medical conditions. We all have positive aspects of our health which we can think about.

I have just watched a recorded interview with a 23 year old, Sevvy Ballesteros, the famous Spanish golfer. Brian Moore, the interviewer, asked him if he thought his bad back was going to cause him problems in his golfing career. I loved Sevvy's answer. He said if he had bad hands, or arms, or bad legs that would be much worse, so, "I am happy with my back".

In 2013, the Lancet, the doctors' magazine, reported that low back pain and depression ranked among the top ten greatest contributors to disability in every country, causing more health loss than diabetes, COPD, and asthma combined. Billions of people suffer from untreated cavities in teeth, tension headaches, anaemia, age-related hearing and sight loss, genital herpes, migraine and giant intestinal roundworm.

There has also been a big growth in diabetes (increase of 136%), Alzheimer's disease (92% increase), medication overuse headache (120% increase), and osteoarthritis (75% increase)."

How do you compare with the rest of the world? Millions of people are suffering from some of these illnesses and most of us are not.

Homework

When you find yourself with a fairly free mind e.g. on a bus, drinking a cup of tea, walking around town, going to sleep, driving to work, cleaning your home etc, take your mind to the things that are going well in your life, the positive things that have happened, the successes you have had, the good parts of your health, the closeness of your friends or family, the reasons you love certain people.

Appreciate all the little things other people do which make your life better.

Chapter 7

Looking outwards

Bad habit: I spend too much of my time looking inwards

Our heads are fascinating places, full of mysteries, questions, opinions about ourselves, memories, fears, worries, all kinds of emotion etc. But the world out there, full of people, opportunities, challenges, love and pleasure, can be a pretty interesting and fun place too. Yes, there are times and events in our lives which take us inside our own heads, but do we want to spend our whole lives in there? It is back to **choice** and most of us know that to spend most or our waking hours looking inward is not a great choice. Many of these thoughts are negative, and they change nothing, and you have had them before.

Some of us even find comfort in this way of living, because it is familiar to us. It is what we know: it is safe and we know what will happen there. It is how we have always done things. If we get outside we might have to show our vulnerabilities to other people. This chapter is about breaking this pattern. This is where the courage comes in.

I am writing about a stereotype here and I am very aware that we are all different. But I have learned these things from people in my groups over and over again. They report that their worlds have become smaller, that they don't go out so much, or get involved with other people like they used to, or get absorbed in some hobby or interest. Lots of people express dissatisfaction with their lifestyle, too much TV, too many glasses of wine, boredom, weight gain and negativity.

Here's some tough love

In the introduction to this book, I wrote about my time locked in my own house, swilling negative thoughts around my head and generally feeling sorry for myself. In a way, I was playing the role of victim.

I invited my friend around one evening, a very straight talking friend. He asked me how I was and I started telling him how miserable and lonely I was. Suddenly he interrupted and said, 'What are you doing about it?' I had no answer. Then, quite firmly, he said, 'What are you complaining to me for if you are not doing anything about it yourself?' He was right. I was wallowing in my own misery and not doing anything to change it. The next day, I joined a dating agency, and put a notice on the staff notice board asking if anyone was interested in playing badminton after work. Five people responded to the badminton notice and I will keep my dating agency secrets to myself. Suddenly, I had a life.

Eight million people in the UK now live alone. Of course some of them are quite happy, but a report from the Office of National Statistics in 2019 noted that "when it comes to well-being, those living on their own report lower levels of happiness and higher levels of anxiety." My guess is it's often not the living alone that does it but the reluctance or shyness or inability (caused by disability) to go out or invite people in. We get stuck in the same patterns.

A 2010 study, reported in the American Scientific Journal, analysed 148 studies covering 300,000 people in the 20th century. It concluded that **regular contacts with friends, family and even colleagues, turns out to be just as good for survival as giving up a 15 cigarette a day habit......................and social networks are more crucial to physical health than exercising or beating obesity'**. Social people are generally (not every individual) happier and physically healthier.

We can see above that social interaction is great for our physical health and quality of life. We could try to get out more, or find some other way of being more social, like inviting people to our place. This is easy to say but harder to do. You have to break an old habit that you have got used to. It means you have got to show yourself, to put your head above the parapet, to break out of your chains and to take a few risks. But ask yourself, 'What is the worst that can happen?'

And if you are worried about turning up alone to these things, ask a friend or relative to go with you, or just arrange to meet one person at a time to start with.

How do I improve my social life? Here are a few ideas.

Phone a friend.

The best way to start building a social life is to start with people you already know.

In her book, 'The Top Five Regrets of the Dying', which I mentioned in the 'Me Time' chapter, Bronnie Ware said that No. 4 regret was '**I wish I had stayed in touch with my friends**'. We all know it. We all say things like, 'I wonder what happened to so and so. I wonder if X still lives in this area. I'd love to meet up with him/her again.' And meeting someone you know is much easier than meeting a bunch of strangers. You have got lots in common and lots of news to catch up on.

You might have to become a bit of a detective and use a phone book, or Facebook (or other social media), or pop down the library to check the electoral register, or phone someone who might know where your friend is.

Or it may not be a friend: it could be a relative. But in the end it comes down to you picking up a phone and making a call, or sending a written message. You have to take some decisive action. Go for it.

When people have done this on my courses, the response has been excellent. Of course, not everybody tries to contact someone, but those who did almost always came to the next class full of stories and enthusiasm for what they had done. Wendy, a woman in one of my groups was a carer. She went back to see one of her ex-clients whom she had got on well with. Both of them were delighted to meet up again. Wendy was beaming when she told us about her visit which all resulted from one phone call. Another woman, in my very first group, got in touch with an old school friend. Now she has an alternative to sitting home alone. I have found that women are much better at doing this than men. Come on, men. Have a go.

Don't be shy: track someone down and arrange to meet. Write it on your list of things to do. It's fun.

There was a song by Andy Williams called Solitaire. One of the lines says, 'While life goes on around me everywhere, I'm playing solitaire.' Is life going on around you? Are you playing solitaire? For many, not all of us, it is a **choice** we make. It doesn't have to be this way.

(I know it is difficult for some people to get out of their houses.)

Me Time.

Go back to the 'Me Time' chapter. Start thinking about getting involved in something outside of your home, maybe, something which is going to stretch you a little, take you out of your inner comfort zone, introduce you to new people, maybe learn some new skills.

Help somebody

We like to feel good about ourselves, but, often, we are so bombed out by daily living that few opportunities present themselves. Many of you reading this book may be wishing that you felt better about yourselves, that your self-esteem was a little higher.

You regular readers of social media will have seen many lists (memes) posted of ways to improve your life.

Many of these lists recommend you to get involved in caring for or helping someone else.

The Happiness Manifesto, a BBC programme, advised viewers to 'Be kind to someone daily.'

The Dalai Lama says the most important thing we can do in life is help other people.

How does helping someone else benefit us?

- We are getting away from our own problems while we focus on someone else.

- We will be appreciated by someone.

- We will be improving someone else's life.

- We are going to feel better about ourselves because we are doing something unselfish and good.

- You are looking outward, away from yourself.

- What help can I give? A chat, do some shopping for them, tidy the garden, the house, maybe paint something, read aloud to them, clean the cooker, take stuff to the tip, take them for a drive, a walk, a coffee, invite them to yours, give them a lift to the hospital, the library, to a friend's house, go through some old photos. Ask them what they would like to do.

Some Positive Stories

My experience when teaching my classes has been that, as people get around halfway through the course they start to make more positive noises and begin to make their lives bigger and look outwards more. Positive thoughts start to take over the negative ones which they used to let take them over. In the first ever group I taught, one person started learning ukulele and then organised a ukulele group and booked a regular teacher: another started a women's social group by advertising in the local free magazine; another gave up her usual Christmas with a relative (which she didn't enjoy) in order to fulfil her dream to serve the homeless. (She was 84 years old.) And another retired person had always wanted to learn Italian, so she decided to rent a flat in Italy for six months. A student I taught organised a dining out group and each week she met with her new group of friends and they went out together. Two women in another class formed a walking group.

Overthinking

When we overthink, it means we are thinking too much. Maybe we are worrying about something we have planned, and we spend too much time thinking about what could go wrong. Or maybe you spend too much time analysing your past. Maybe you have a friend who you like to overanalyse with. Maybe you spend your time wishing you were different and wondering why you are like you are. And this overthinking can trigger all kinds of emotions which are better left alone like anger, guilt, shame, regret, resentment or fear. Do you really want to be feeling these things? Will anything change as a result of your overthinking? Have you been doing this for a long time with no visible success?

We have heard all of this before when we were talking about negative thinking. Nothing changes, you do it over and over again, and it generally makes you miserable. And you never get to a final answer. So is it time to stop doing this?

How can we stop overthinking?

Not all of this list will apply to you. Choose the ones that do and work on them.

- **Recognise what you are doing**. Know your enemy, your unnecessary thoughts. Spend the next few days asking yourself when and where you overthink. What do you overthink about? How often do you repeat the same overthinking on the same subject? Do you share your overthinking with someone else? What good do these thoughts do? When do they end? How many times have you solved a problem by overthinking? By all means, think, but know when you have done enough. Stop going round in circles.

- **Get your mind away from your past.** It has happened and you cannot change it. Leave it behind and focus on the present. I know some terrible things have happened and you can't let go of them instantly. The worse they were, the longer it takes and the more stubborn the memories. But remind yourself, as you try to let them go, that your bad thoughts are changing nothing. You had them yesterday and last week. Notice what you are doing and take your thoughts to another place. The more you practise this, the longer will be the gaps between your unpleasant thoughts.

- **Stop analysing yourself and other people**. You are not a psychiatrist. You never get to a final answer or explanation. You keep looking for reasons to explain your or other people's behaviour. And the next day you think of another explanation. Psychiatrists can take five years or more to get to the bottom of a person's problems, and they are experts. Just stop doing it. Your questions and answers are not going to change anything.

- **The future hasn't happened yet.** There are some things you cannot change no matter how much you think of them. When you feel anxious about the future, try to bring yourself back into the present e.g. do a breathing or relaxation exercise. Change your activity. Or maybe do some exercise. Get into what you are doing: get yourself into the present.

- **Mind readers are seldom right**. We cannot read minds. We do not **KNOW** what other people are thinking but we often **GUESS**, and, mostly, our guesses are wrong. An acquaintance walks past you without catching your eye and looking miserable. And some of us are thinking, 'Oh dear, have I done something wrong?' or 'How rude'. But maybe the guy just had something heavy on his mind and genuinely didn't see you. We don't know, so stop reading minds. You never know what difficulties other people are dealing with. Accept that people behave differently at different times and their behaviour is not always predictable.

- **Stop trying to control everything**. Trust people. Ask them for help and then trust them to do the job. You cannot cover every possibility especially when other people are involved. A young mother in one of my classes had entrusted her small child to her mother for the two hour class, checking her phone for messages and calling her during the ten minute break. Eventually the worry became too much and she stopped attending class. All because she was overthinking.....what if, what if?

- **Don't give yourself such a hard time** Many of us have an inner critic who is always finding fault in us. 'I shouldn't have done this. I could have done that better. It was my fault. I am no good.' This inner critic is usually a voice from your past which you have held onto, another person's opinion of you, not yours to begin with. You weren't born with low opinions of yourself. Somebody put them there. We mentioned it briefly in Unit 2. And you let the voice say what it wants, and you remember it and believe it. Do you really want this inner critic inside you? No, of course not, because it is not your voice. Sure, we fail at things but that doesn't turn our complete self into something bad. You could try laughing at it when you hear its voice or maybe just tell it to clear off (or something stronger). Anyway it is not your voice and you are not interested in what it says. This is the type of thought you don't want, so let it pass through like the champagne bubbles. Don't hold onto it.

Procrastination

I left writing this section until the very last minute. It had been playing on my mind for ages, but I just couldn't get down to writing it. Other things were getting in the way, football matches, friends calling, and I love physical work in the garden. And when I found myself with free time, I just wasn't in a writing mood. Now I am worried that I am going to leave things out and I am getting anxious. Maybe it won't turn out to be good enough to put in the book. I'm rushing it and I know I will make some stupid mistakes like leaving words out, not putting in the correct punctuation etc, and I just won't be satisfied with it. I wish I had started it earlier and done a proper job.

Negative thinking people often tend to be procrastinators. Procrastination is all about putting things off, not getting jobs done, or not having conversations, that you have been wanting or needing to do. These are things outside of yourself that you need to engage with. And a voice inside you is saying, 'I wish I could get those jobs out of the way'. Sometimes it is quite an important, even urgent, job, and you still don't get around to doing it. Maybe you are a student who has left your assignment to the last minute. Or, like me, you have got a load of paperwork that needs to be dealt with. And of course there are other jobs, too, more things that you will do 'tomorrow'. And as they build up, they start to weigh you down, and cause you stress which can make you negative.

You hear people saying things like: 'I must take that stuff to the dump, I must get that essay done, I have been meaning to paint that door, clean that window, call the dentist, start my diet, get my car serviced, phone my auntie, I must talk to my neighbour about that sensitive problem, do my tax form, for ages. I wish I could find the time. I just can't seem to get round to it.'

How can you feel content if you have always got these jobs hanging over you that you just can't seem to get done? They nag away at you. We are trying to get rid of thoughts that get us down. Think of the relief you feel when you have got an important job out of the way.

Here are a few tips to get yourself more organised.

- **Make a list, make a list, make a list.** Lists are brilliant. Once you have written a job down, it becomes a lot more real. And you don't have to worry about remembering the job because it is there, written down asking to be done. But you do have to remember to look at the list.

- **Set times to do things, make a timetable.** Write a time schedule on your list. Call doctor at 9.30 tomorrow morning, Go to DIY shop on way home from work tonight. Call Auntie Ada at 8p.m.

- **Choose the item on your list that you least want to do** and get it done. Quite often these are important and you have been waiting to do them for some time. In my case, it is paperwork jobs that I put off. You will feel a load lifted from your mind when that job is done. We looked at priorities earlier. Things which are urgent need to be done **now**.

- **Get started** You don't have to finish the job, just get it started. Once the ball is rolling it moves much easier. Get the things ready that you need to get started, tools, equipment, pens, paper, forms etc. Then start the job.

- **Break it down into manageable pieces** if it is a big job, You don't have to do it all in one go. I'll strip the paint off the door today at 11. I'll do the undercoat at 11 tomorrow. I'll do the top coat at 11 the next day. And on the fourth day, I will admire my handiwork and feel pleased with myself. Another job out of the way. Very satisfying.

- **Try a change of scenery**. Get away from the TV, the favourite armchair, I-Phone, laptop, kids, friends, music, snacks etc. Most of the time we don't have a good reason for not doing something. But we often have excuses, for example, Errol rang; I had a headache and needed a lie down; I forgot; I couldn't find the right screwdriver; I will do it tomorrow; I was watching some wildlife programme. Get real with yourself. Recognise when you are putting things off for no good reason. Give yourself a good talking to.

- **It doesn't have to be perfect.** There is a big difference between, 'I can't do it perfectly' and 'I can't do it at all'. Striving for perfection in everything can drive you crazy. If it works, it is generally fine. You don't have to gold plate it, or make sure all the loose ends are exactly the same length.

Homework

Phone a friend or relative whom you haven't seen for a while. Arrange to meet.

Make a list of your priorities. Make time for the ones at the top of your list.

Look at the people close to you and see if anyone needs your support. Lots of people need help with shopping or practical jobs around the house, or just a chat with a friendly face.

Invite someone to your home for a chat or a game of something.

You will remember that there are a number of other suggestions in the 'me time' chapter.

Make a list of all of the jobs you have been putting off. Decide which ones are top priority. Timetable them. Do them. Do the one you least want to do first. Build yourself a schedule and stick to it.

Chapter 8

Learn a positive description of yourself

Bad habit: we get used to seeing ourselves in negative terms

People who think negative thoughts generally find it hard to talk positively about themselves. This can be quite limiting when applying for jobs, going to interviews or writing your profile on a dating website, for example. Negative thinking people may not even accept they have good sides to their character. I was one of those people: my job applications were terrible. A common interview question is, 'What are your strengths?' It is important and useful for you to be able to talk about yourself in positive terms.

In this chapter, I am going to suggest that you do a character strengths survey, online, which will tell you what your character strengths are. This survey was compiled by Martin Seligman, the father of Positive Psychology, and his colleague Christopher Peterson in collaboration with 55 top social scientists. It is top of the range. They worked out 24 positive character strengths which are common to people everywhere. We all have them. Then, they formulated a series of questions which would reveal which were your strongest character traits from 1 down to 24.

I have done this exercise with some of my groups. One lady went straight to the bottom of her list when her results came back. She told me she wanted to iron out her problems and improve her weaknesses in order to become a better person. I explained to her that as she improved any weaknesses and moved them up the list, others would take their place at the bottom and she would spend her life trying to put right all the things that she thought were wrong with her. Wouldn't it be better, I asked, if she focussed on the top of her list and saw herself as a bunch of strengths rather than a collection of weaknesses?

I did the survey myself and when my own list came back, the following were at at the top: sense of humour, creativity, leadership, kindness, honesty, social intelligence, bravery. These are who I am. These are my special strengths. These are how I should see myself and describe myself to others. OK, there are a lot of really enviable character traits that are not in my top eight like love and forgiveness. But they don't want you to spend your life focussing on what you are not so strong at. They want you to say this is me: these top 6,7 or 8 special strengths are who I am.

You have got to answer these survey questions honestly. You can't fiddle your answers to the questions and try to get the results to say you are a loving, kind, gorgeous and perfect person. They have got all kinds of tricks, cross-checks etc to prevent that.

The list, my 24 strengths in order, came as a surprise to me. For example, I had never really given myself any credit for being a kind person, and kindness came in at No 4, so it's one of my special strengths 'Why?', I asked myself. I started to look at my life and when I had been kind. There were lots of examples. I had been more likely to think of bad things I had done, than give myself credit for good things. My opinion of myself went up when I spent time thinking about my strengths.

So, doing this questionnaire/survey can help you like yourself more. It can tell you why you should feel positive about yourself. Some of my group members have described this as a 'light bulb moment'. They said it was great to find a positive way of describing themselves. It made them see themselves in a different way.

The Positive Thinking people are not concerned at all with character weaknesses. All twenty four character traits on the list are strengths, but, for all of us, some are stronger than others, the special strengths. You can do this questionnaire free of charge and get your own list of your character strengths if you go online to: www.viacharacter.org/survey/account/register

* I have absolutely no connection with this organisation, financial or otherwise.

If you don't have a computer, maybe you can find a relative or friend to set this up for you. It is well worth doing. It is easy for them to set it up and easy for you to answer the questions once your relative has shown you how. It takes less than an hour. They will send you your results by email, ranking your character strengths from 1-24. They can send it to your relative's email address. It's an easy way to find out what a great person you are. For extra fees, they will go into more detail about how you can use these character strengths to your benefit but the basic package is free.

Seligman and Peterson suggest that, when your list of strengths comes back, you focus on your top six, seven or eight and you describe yourself in those terms. For example," I am honest, kind, creative, good at judging things, a team player, loving and forgiving." That is who you are. These are your special strengths. This person sounds pretty great.

Or you could go to the bottom of your list and say, for example, you are not so strong at forgiving, not very grateful, have little self-control and you are not great at leading a group. But you still have some strength in these areas just not as much as your special strengths.

Which would you rather be, the first or the second person, the one who describes herself as a list of special strengths or the one who prefers to talk about what she is not so good at? How will you choose to describe yourself? Remember it is a choice. Your choice. Are you going to be positive or negative?

I encourage you to go to the website above, complete the questionnaire, find out what a great person you are, and remind yourself frequently of your special strengths.

Homework

Go to www.viacharacter.org/survey/account/register and complete the survey.

Chapter 9

What have we learned these last few weeks?

We **CAN** control our minds better. We can start to recognise when our minds are slipping into negative thoughts and then switch away.

This means that negative thinking is a choice. We can choose to stay with it or think of more positive thoughts. We know this is not easy at first but it gets easier with practice, just like any other skill.

We weren't born with bad habits. We learned them, and we can unlearn them. Negative thinking is a habit, and, like smoking, it is bad for us. We can give it up.

Thoughts are not facts: they are just ideas and we can decide their fate. Just because negative thoughts are in your head doesn't mean they are true. Let them pass through. Pay them no attention. Hold on to the thoughts that you like, not the ones that make you miserable. Focus your thoughts on what you are doing now.

You have learned a variety of ways to switch away from negativity.

- Remind yourself that repeated negative thinking changes nothing.

- Bring yourself into the present moment. What is happening in your life NOW, in this precise moment?

- Focus on your breathing, relaxing your muscles, walking upright, the things around you, your here and now. Don't just look at your environment. Smell, touch and listen to it.

- Go to your store of happy/positive thoughts or memories and think of one of them if you find yourself getting negative.

- Think gratitude: think about people you like, not dislike. Try to appreciate the good parts in the various aspects of your life like friends, work, family and health, for example.

- Make lists and timetables and get jobs done and out of the way. Then you have less to worry about.

You are important. Your needs, interests and desires are important. You were not put on this planet just to serve others. You are entitled to a slice of the pie. This will require you to be assertive and let people know what you want. Carve out a life for yourself, your 'Me Time'.

Meditation, for 10 minutes, preferably 20, daily, is an excellent way to empty your mind, to release stress, to sharpen your brain, to relax and restore some energy. Regular practice will make you a calmer person.

Use your relaxation exercises to get you off to sleep.

If you can make a habit of these good practices listed above, the quality of your life will improve dramatically. Remember that these bad habits you have won't change overnight.

Chapter 10

Where else can I get support?

This book has been about trying to eliminate negative thinking by changing your behaviour, the things you do and the things you think about. But our negative thinking is often caused by things that happened to us in the past, things which have made us anxious or guilty for example, and, although we have changed our behaviour, the memories of past events still remain. And they still work on our brains.

Sometimes these deep-seated thoughts and feelings will come back and try to take us over again. This can lead to further episodes of negative thinking and we need to be prepared for that. This changing of your thinking habits is not a permanent solution to your negative thinking problems. In the future, events may lead us into negative thoughts again. You have not failed: you have merely slipped back a little and you now need to get back on the bike and start pedalling again. Remind yourself of what you learned in this book. Come back to the book and start to practise those good thinking habits again.

This book is not a cure for anxiety or depression, but it can help you to handle these illnesses much better. There are other things you can do, too. Here are three recommendations I can give you for further support:

- the **NHS has an excellent website** which will point you towards help with all kinds of problems including anxiety, depression, loneliness, bereavement and many others. Here it is:

- www.nhs.uk/conditions/stress-anxiety-depression/

- call your local branch of **MIND** or you could go to the Mind website which will tell you about support available in your local area such as relaxation classes and self-help groups.

- www.mind.org.uk/

- **IAPT** (Improving Access to Psychological Therapies) is another organisation, part of the NHS, which offers a variety of different kinds of support from individual and group therapy through to computer programmes based on Cognitive Behavioural Therapy (CBT) which you can do at home. They do a lot of work with anxiety and depression sufferers. You can now call them direct to make an appointment or ask your GP to do it for you.

I wish you all good luck and positive thoughts.

Tim Harris

Enjoyed this book?

Please consider leaving a review to help others find it.

Printed in Great Britain
by Amazon